Annie
and
Koos
of the Bushveldt

This book is for my grandchildren:
Campbell, Zoe, Rosie, Stella and George
and for all the descendants of
Anna Jacoba Elizabeth Geissler (born Greeff).

It was inspired by the writings of
Jacoba Elizabeth De La Rey (born Greeff)

With thanks to Diana Cucvara,
Joanna Powling and Paul Williams.

Published in 2016 by Elizabeth Williams
takana@bigpond.com

Text copyright © Elizabeth Williams 2016

Illustrations copyright © Virginia Gray 2016

The moral right of the author has been asserted.

National Library of Australia Cataloguing-in-Publication entry has been applied for.

ISBN 978-0-9945552-6-7 (Ingram Spark)

Custom book production by Captain Honey
Cover and internal design by Natalie Winter
www.captainhoney.com.au

5 4 3 2 1   16 17 18 19 20

Annie and Koos

of the Bushveldt

Elizabeth Williams

Illustrations by Virginia Gray

BACK THEN STORIES

Contents

On the Greeff Farm **1**

Leaving Home **4**

Making ready for the Trek **8**

Trekking in the Early Morning **12**

Camping on the Veldt **17**

Christmas **21**

On the Trek Again **24**

The Marico River **28**

An Expedition to Get Wild Honey **31**

Elephant Crossing **35**

Cannon Fire Again **40**

In the Makim Farmhouse **43**

The Very Strange Ghost **46**

Crossing the Harts River **49**

The Night Sky **54**

Leaving the Harts River **58**

Nonnie, Annie and The General **62**

A Bitter Peace, but Peace at Last **66**

CHAPTER 1

On the Greeff Farm

F̲ar away in Africa, O Best Beloved, in a time even before your grandmother lived, we find two children from a large family living on a farm.

They were sister and brother called Annie and Koos and they were older than the three other children in their family. Because their mother was so busy she often said that Annie and Koos must take responsibility for themselves. Thus, Annie and Koos relied on each other for help, and also did many jobs around the farm to help their mother.

Mother needed their help because Father was away fighting the Khaki soldiers. They had to carry the wood for the kitchen fire and buckets of water for washing. Everyday Koos fed the chickens and carefully collected the eggs. When it was sunny and windy, they would hang the washing on the line to dry. They liked being older than the other children and liked to be useful.

But one day Mother said, "Annie and Koos there are some big problems in our country, and I must leave the farm with the other children and travel south to a safe place."

Then Mother said, "Annie and Koos I cannot take you with me, you must go to your Aunt Nonnie who loves you very much. You will go with Nonnie and your cousins on her wagon and travel north, away from the Khaki soldiers."

Annie and Koos did not understand what was wrong with their country but they did know there were soldiers called Khakis travelling over the land and taking farms. They burned the fruit trees and took all the food for themselves. Sometimes they burned the farmhouses. That was the reason

Father was fighting with the Commandos against the Khakis.

Both the children did not want to leave their home and leave their family. Now, they did not like being the eldest in the family and wished that they also were too young to leave their mother.

Koos said, "But, but Mumma we don't want to go away from you." And he cried.

Annie tried to be brave and said that she would take care of Koos while they were with Nonnie on her wagon. The tears were inside her but she didn't let them out. She tried not to think of the day they would have to leave.

CHAPTER 2

Leaving Home

Now the day arrived, when Annie and Koos were to leave their farm and their mother, and their two little brothers and baby sister. They were very sad about this but were also busy getting some of their favourite things to take with them.

In her canvas bag Annie put her doll whom she called Polly. Polly was all floppy and raggedy from being carried everywhere in Annie's apron. But Annie was very fond of Polly because she belonged to her since she was a tiny girl.

She also had something else that was very precious to her; a drawing book and six coloured pencils. Annie liked to draw animals and birds. It made her happy to think that perhaps while she was travelling with Nonnie on the wagon she would see different animals and birds that she could draw.

Meanwhile Koos made his own plans. The first thing he put in his canvas bag was his slingshot and some smooth river stones. On his birthday Father had helped him make the sling and showed him how to place a stone in it. Then, he showed him how to aim the stone and fling it with force at a hyena. Koos practised until he was a good shot. It made him feel powerful like a hunter.

Koos also decided to take his pet chicken, Cluck. He could not leave her behind because when the Khaki soldiers came they would eat her for dinner. He didn't know how he could take her because Nonnie had her own favourite chickens that she would take. Then, Koos remembered down by the shed there was an old brown sack. Perfect he thought!

Mother took Annie and Koos in her carriage to Nonnie's place and it was here that they said goodbye to her and the other children. When Annie and Koos started to cry, Nonnie came and put her plump arms around them.

She held them close to her and said, "Tomorrow we begin our big trek north away from my farm and away from the Khaki soldiers. I will need you both to help me feed the chickens, collect the eggs and hang the washing as we travel along. Your cousins will have other jobs to do, but I know you can help me with these jobs."

Nonnie was kind but she was also strict and Koos felt nervous about secretly smuggling Cluck. But he knew she had to come with him.

Mother gave them a large soft parcel. They

wondered what was inside but had to wait until the next day to open it.

After hugging Mumma and kissing the baby, they watched the carriage going away down the dusty road. Mumma looked back at her children one last time. Then, in the distance, she saw that Annie had one bag but Koos had one bag and a sack.

Why had Koos got a sack, she wondered.

The children picked up their bags and went into Nonnie's house.

CHAPTER 3

Making Ready for the Trek

The next day, before the sun rose and, in the darkness, they prepared for the trek north. From their bed Annie and Koos saw the dark shape of the two covered wagons and they saw two of their older cousins, Jan and Susanna, already packing food into boxes and rounding up the milking cows and the chickens that would go with them.

Nonnie knew that they would need milk and

eggs on their great journey, so she was taking these animals with them.

Koos saw Nonnie, jumped out of bed and said, "Nonnie, I'll catch the chickens and put them in the big wicker basket. I'm good at catching chickens and I have a big sack to put them in."

Nonnie agreed and Koos ran outside carrying his sack. Looking out the kitchen window, Annie saw Koos chasing the chickens, pouncing and popping them into his sack. What a lot of squawking and squealing there was. Finally all the chickens were caught and Koos put them into the very large basket cage which was put on the wagon. He could see Cluck peeping through. How proud Koos was of himself!

Annie went with Nonnie and her cousin Susanna to the kitchen to pack the things they would need to make bread and make stews for their dinner. They must take pots and pans, tin plates, mugs and canteens for water and milk. Also flour, dried meat, beans coffee, corn, sugar and dried fruit.

A large tent was also loaded onto one of the wagons and canvas stretched over the top of the frames. At the front of each wagon were four huge oxen. They were very large and strong because they

needed to pull the heavy wagons behind them over rough tracks and deep gullies.

The children watched as the oxen had yokes placed over their necks. Each pair of oxen was yoked to the other by a piece of wood and the yokes were fixed to a pole between the oxen. This was attached to the wagon which was pulled forward when the oxen walked.

Later that morning all was ready to go. Nonnie

climbed to the front of the first wagon with the driver, Inkoshi, who had a whip. He shouted as he cracked the whip over the heads of the oxen, then the wagons moved forward. The great trek to escape the Khakis had begun

It was December 1900 and the bright sun was rising in the sky.

CHAPTER 4

Trekking in the Early Morning

After packing, the weary children trudged alongside the wagons. The wagons were so heavy with all the stores and the oxen were pulling ever so hard, but they were still only moving slowly.

Nonnie sat high on the wagon with Inkoshi the driver, and the second wagon followed not far behind. After a while, Koos ran ahead of the first wagon and Annie ran after him. Annie looked sad, and Koos darted here and there looking for insects and grubs.

Annie warned Koos, "You're crazy Koos, you should be careful that Nonnie does not become suspicious about Cluck. Otherwise we might eat him for dinner tonight. She will be so angry with you."

But Koos laughed at his sister. He found more insects and put them in his pocket as quickly as he could. He couldn't wait for Cluck to gobble those tockie tock beetles but he would have to wait until they made camp that night. Then he would give Cluck such a feast!

Annie found Green Pigeon feathers. Before putting them in her pocket, she looked carefully at the colours and thought that nothing could be prettier than the shiny greens and yellows. Maybe she would see a Green Pigeon soon. That would cheer her up.

Koos kicked at the dusty track and Annie bowed her head as she thought about her mother and family so far away.

Nonnie called to Annie and Koos and said they could ride on her wagon for a while because they were tired. They climbed up the wagon wheels and sat close to Nonnie who sang to them as they moved along. But one tockie tock beetle crawled out of Koos's pocket and, quickly, before Nonnie saw it Koos squashed it and put it in his pocket again. That was lucky!

As the sun rose higher in the sky, it became so very hot that Nonnie said it was time to stop. She told Inkoshi, the driver, to stop the wagon so he dropped the reins and his whip. Msizi, the other driver, followed, and the oxen were unyoked. The oxen team was outspanned so they could roam in search of grass.

In the shade of the wagons they ate lunch and drank water from the canteen. Nonnie had made

mealie biscuits for them to eat. They ate them with some dried meat while they listened to Nonnie's plan,

"We've made a good start today. We'll stay here tonight and put our tent up under the Marula trees until early morning. Then we must set out again tomorrow to get away from the Khaki's. They are not far behind us. We don't want to be captured and put in a prison camp, so we must press on. We must go toward the mountains which are a few days travel from here."

Annie, Koos and all the cousins knew that they must cooperate if they were to escape the Khakis and must do all that they could to help.

So, it was that all the children, Inkoshi and Msizi and the herders all worked together to put up the tents and to get provisions for the camp. Annie felt so tired, but she and Susanna carried the camp beds, while Koos let the chickens free to peck at the dry grass until sunset.

CHAPTER 5

Camping on the Veldt

Never before had the children camped out at night, and they did feel frightened. Frightened of the lions which they knew roamed the veldt. But they were also excited to be outside and to be with their cousins on this big adventure.

The sun, like a great fiery ball, set in the west.

It was time for the chickens to be brought into the safety of the coop and Koos chased them once more

popping them into his sack. Nonnie watched him and thought what a good boy! But she counted the chickens and thought how strange that there were thirteen chickens in the coop when she only brought twelve. But, she had too many things to think about to then worry about one extra chicken. She did not see Koos reach into his pocket for the squashed beetles and she did not hear him say.

"Cluck, my pet, here is a treat for you, delicious tockie tock beetles."

As the blanket of darkness fell over the camp, a fire was lit between the wagons. Here Nonnie, the children

and the helpers cooked dinner and sat around the fire singing songs while Jan played his harmonica. They gazed up at the fantastic sky with the millions of bright stars. It made Annie feel so small, but so lucky to be able to see such a beautiful sight.

That night she and Koos were to share the same camp bed, so they sat alongside each other and opened the brown paper parcel. Inside was a quilt that Mumma had made for them with a pattern of different birds and chickens all over it. There was a beautiful wood pigeon made with green and yellow colours just like the colours in the feather that Annie had found. And there was a chicken made from red material which looked just like Cluck.

Not too far away they heard wild animals calling and lions roaring to each other and Koos whispered to Annie, "Don't worry. The animals are frightened of fire, and our camp fire will burn all night, until we get up in the morning."

The children snuggled down and slept soundly until the first rays of sun came through the flap of the tent. They washed quickly in a bucket of water and Koos walked around the outside of their camp. Sure enough he found spoor, the footprints of lions in the sandy soil. Later as he packed he put his slingshot in his pocket, just in case.

The wagons were loaded again, the milking cows were sent ahead with the herders and the teams set off in the direction of the mountains near the Marico River.

CHAPTER 6

Christmas

Many days followed and the days were getting hotter. Every day on the trek was very much like the first day, with Koos searching for grubs and beetles whenever he could and Annie sitting on the wagon with Nonnie and Inkoshi.

Sometimes Annie sat alongside Inkoshi and they liked to talk. Annie had known Inkoshi since she was a very little girl because she had visited Nonnie's farm many times and met him there. She liked him very much. He had dark skin and curly hair and was very tall and strong although he was not young any more.

Inkoshi promised Annie he would help her find some interesting birds when they came nearer to the Marico River. Inkoshi knew so much about animals, birds and plants. He would be such a help to Annie and she felt happy to talk to him as they trekked along the dusty track. He also told Annie about many plants that could be used to cure sickness. She listened carefully to all the things he told her.

They travelled on until one very hot day they came to a farm house which had been burned down, all except for one room which still had a roof. The Khakis had destroyed most of this house, and the family had gone, perhaps to a prison camp.

"Let us stop here," said Nonnie. "There is some shelter and we are all so very tired. Look, there is vegetable garden and some fruit trees. Oh Koos, set the chickens free. Children, see what vegetables you can find for dinner and Inkoshi and Msizi, unyoke the oxen. If we are comfortable here we could stay until Christmas."

They stayed for a few days in this room of the burned farmhouse. But just before Christmas a wagon with another family with a wagon joined them, also seeking safety from the Khakis.

They all gathered around the campfire on Christmas Eve to sing and play games under the stars. It was a happy time for all the wanderers with plenty of good food to eat. All too soon, the other family loaded their wagon and left.

The sound of cannons could be heard in the distance. The fighting was not so far from where they were, so Nonnie said they must up and go again on the long trek towards the Marico River and the mountains.

CHAPTER 7

On the Trek Again

A s the sun rose, the wanderers gathered their belongings to put on the wagon. Inkoshi found the tarpaulin folded near the back of the wagon and called Koos to help him to attach it to the wagon.

Then he spied something very long and dark lying in a fold of the tarpaulin. Very slowly, and saying, 'beware,' Inkoshi backed away from the huge snake and pulled Koos with him. As they moved away, the

mamba snake woke, and lifted its head high to stare at them. Inkoshi called to Nonnie to throw him his rifle from the back of the wagon. Quickly he aimed the gun as the mamba slithered swiftly towards them. Koos felt his heart thumping, and he tried not to panic. The gun cracked as Inkoshi pulled the trigger. Koos closed his eyes and when he opened them the mamba was there lying at his feet, dead.

The children had heard many stories about the deadly black mamba but they had never seen one before. Shocked but curious, the children approached the dead snake. They stood around it in a circle, Annie held Koos's hand while Inkoshi spread out its long brown body and opened its mouth. The inside of its mouth was inky black. Now they understood why it was called the black mamba.

As the wagons left, the wanderers could see the hungry hyenas attacking the body of the dead snake, pulling it this way and that as they squabbled over their share.

They continued along the dusty track toward the mountains with the booming of cannon fire not far behind them. So they trekked along day, after day, camping out at night. Months had passed since Christmas and the weather was no longer so hot and the nights were cooler.

The children accepted that this is the way they must exist until the war was over. As the months passed they felt homesick for their farm, but they knew they could not return yet. Sometimes they felt hungry but they understood that Nonnie was doing her best to give them whatever she could. While the cows were with them they had fresh milk, when the chickens laid eggs they would have an omelette.

Time passed slowly until at last, after many weeks, they approached the Marico River. All the wanderers were weary and wished to rest. It was here that they felt safe from the sound of war. At least for a while.

CHAPTER 8

The Marico River

As the wanderers approached the river, the dusty dry dirt, scrubby bushes, and stubbly grass ended. Now there were enormous shady trees, cool air, lush grass and the sound of water spilling over rocks.

"Let us make camp here until we have to move," said Nonnie."It is so peaceful and I can't hear the sound of cannons, so we must be far away from the Khakis now. However, we need to take care because there are many wild animals that come to the river to drink and they could be a danger to us."

The tent was set up under the trees and the things were taken from the wagon to make life as comfortable as possible. Nonnie needed an oven to bake bread, so Inkoshi dug a deep hole into the side of the riverbank. The children watched as he lit a fire inside the hole then set a rack above the ashes. Nonnie made the bread mixture, kneaded it and then formed it into a loaf shape. She then placed the loaf above the rack. It worked like a true oven.

The first night at the river was such fun. Inkoshi and Msizi built a huge fire. The children could smell the fresh bread in the oven and felt as hungry as hunters. Nonnie made a chicken casserole, which was so delicious the children could not think of anything better to eat. Then Nonnie looked at them and said, "Well that was a good dinner, chicken is always so tasty. I'll wait until the baby chicks grow and then we can have another feast."

Koos did not like the sound of this and feared that Cluck might be the next chicken dinner. Not my pet chicken, he thought!

Earlier that day, Inkoshi had seen tiny honey birds flying through the trees and he knew there was wild honey to be found not too far away. He explained that if they followed a honey bird it would lead them to a hive. When he told the children about this, they begged Nonnie to let them make an expedition into the tall trees to find it. How they were longing for something sweet to eat.They called out at the tops of their voices, "We want honey, we want honey."

CHAPTER 9

An Expedition to get Wild Honey

So it was that the next morning while it was still cool, Msizi and all the children left the camp and wandered amongst the trees looking for where the wild honey could be found. Msizi was not surprised that before long a little honey bird flew just in front of them and called, flying back to where they were

and then leading them on. Msizi knew the ways of the honey bird and how they led people to the bees' hive. He knew it would want a honey reward for taking them there.

The little bird flew to a tree and called, flapping its wings. It wasn't difficult to see that there was a hollow about half way up the trunk, and there were a lot of bees buzzing about it.

Koos wanted that honey, but he thought he might let someone else get it.

He thought his older cousin Jan should climb the tree.

"Jan, you are the best climber. Your legs are much longer than mine, so up you go."

Jan said, "No way, I'm not going to climb the tree with those stinging bees buzzing about." The children argued about who should climb the tree. They all wanted honey, but no one was brave enough to try.

Feeling miserable, the children returned to camp squabbling all the way. The girls said the boys were useless and the boys called them sissies. They were so glum that night that no singing in the world would make them happy.

The only child who was a bit happy was Annie because she'd seen the honey bird and now, while its image was fresh in her mind, she did some drawings and was quite pleased with them. So pleased that she signed her name at the bottom of the page.

The next morning Inkoshi said, "Let us go back to the hive now. I have a plan which will probably stop the bees from stinging us."

Back to the tree they went with the honey bird

leading the way. Inkoshi lit a fire in a tin can and burned some green leaves. Clouds of smoke rose from the can and then Inkoshi hung the can on a branch so that the wind would blow the smoke straight into the hive. All that smoke calmed the bees.

Jan climbed the tree trunk, then put his hand into the hollow. The bees were buzzing about him, but they didn't try to sting him. The smoke was in his eyes but he could still feel the honey comb inside the hollow and he pulled it out, putting a big hunk into the tin can. Then down he came.

The honey bird flitted about chirping and begging for some honey so Jan gave it the first small piece of the comb. The yellow honey was so sweet and delicious. They all dipped their eager fingers in and licked their fingers with delight.

CHAPTER 10

Elephant Crossing

From the campsite the wanderers could hear many animals during the day and at night. One of the animal sounds they could hear was an elephant and it didn't seem far away. Inkoshi said he could take them exploring further up the river. Of course, Inkoshi did have a gun just in case it was needed; not to shoot the elephants but to shoot any other animal that may approach them with a hungry look.

They set off early walking along the riverbank. A mist hung over the river and, as they trudged along, they saw hippos resting in the water with their nostrils just above the waterline. What a way to keep cool! Koos wished that he could be a hippopotamus resting in the cool water, but what about the terror beneath the water? Koos started to think about crocodiles and how they would eat a little boy like him in a flash of their big jaws.

A moment later Susanna shrieked, "Crocodile, crocodile!"

The children huddled together as something moved through the reeds on the river's edge just in front of them. It pushed through the reeds to the

edge of the water. For one moment it stood on the bank, then in a flash it plunged into the river.

" That's too small to be a crocodile, Inkoshi said. "It is a water lizard called a lagavaan and is harmless."

They then saw many lagavaans as they followed the river. They were no longer afraid but they did keep their distance. All the while as they trudged along they could hear the elephants trumpeting getting louder. This meant they were getting closer. They turned a corner in the path and there, not far in the distance, they saw the elephants.

There were twelve of them, including a young one and another very small one. Most of them were having a splendid time in the river. Some were in

deeper water spurting from their trunks, while others were closer to the edge rolling in the mud and sloshing it over their bodies and heads.

Annie was most interested in the mother elephant with her young one that was on the grass close to the edge. She found an old log to sit on and took out her sketchbook. She turned over a page where she'd drawn the honey bird and made some quick sketches of the mother and baby elephant.

Further along the riverbank and on the opposite side, the children saw a very large herd of elephants walking towards the water. They were walking one behind the other. The lead elephant entered the deep river and the others followed, one by one, going deeper into the swift flowing water. Deeper and deeper they went until the children were amazed to see them swimming.

Koos wondered how such enormous, heavy animals could swim. But that is exactly what they were doing. The river was very deep in the middle and so they swam, lifting their trunks into the air to breathe.

Koos said," I want to remember this for ever, and I wish all my family were here to see this, but Annie can do some drawings to show them when we're back together. Otherwise they won't believe me."

What an amazing sight to see. The lead elephant swam until she reached the riverbank on the other side, and the others followed. As they came out of the water they grazed on the soft grass near the river and then they continued to lumber on, leaving the river behind them. They took no notice of the smaller group of elephants playing in the mud, nor of the children and Inkoshi. Gradually, they became a grey smudge and disappeared into the distance.

CHAPTER 11

Cannon Fire Again

T he children returned to the camp and started to do the chores which they hadn't done earlier in the day. Nonnie was busy making candles, which they needed because stores were running low. As they were working, there came the booming sound of cannon fire in the distance. Nonnie stopped work and ordered everyone to pack up the tent, the cooking gear, the camp beds and all their equipment on to the wagons. Koos went in search of the chickens that were pecking around the campsite and put them into the large cage as quickly as he could. Msizi loaded it onto the wagon.

The oxen were harnessed to the wagons and Inkoshi and Msizi took their whips and cracked them urgently over their heads. The wanderers were moving again, away from the Marico River.

The sun was setting as they moved down the track and darkness was approaching. They did not feel sad about leaving the river because they knew they just had to move. Nobody complained about what was happening. They needed to keep out of harm's way. The moon was shining now like a huge yellow lantern in the sky and they continued on their way until midnight. Then Nonnie said, "The oxen will need to rest for a couple of hours, then we will move on again. We absolutely must."

Everyone needed rest so the tent was put up quickly. In the tent Koos and Annie were scared so they huddled together under their warm quilt. And in the dark, they whispered to each other.

"Let's think about home and let's dream we are there and maybe it will come true. Nonnie prays a lot for our safety and I think God listens to her," said Annie.

They slept for only a short time, and then they got up from their bed ready to travel on. It was still dark as the wagons moved on down the trek in the moonlight.

At the break of day, they could see in the distance a farmhouse close to some thorn bushes. Here they would stay for as long as it was safe away from the sound of cannon fire. It had once been the farmhouse of the Makin family. Fortunately the kitchen in the farmhouse had not been destroyed by fire. Nonnie made a tasty dinner for all the hungry children.

CHAPTER 12

In the Makim Farmhouse

It felt so strange to be in someone else's house using their kitchen, sitting in their chairs and thinking about where the family might be now. It was a big house, and it had not been completely destroyed. The children thought it was a bit spooky sleeping in the bedrooms where another family had slept.

After dinner and after Nonnie had said prayers, the children told each other ghost stories. When Jan told the others about the ghost of the spotted panther they could see its yellow eyes staring at them in the gloom. They all had to stomp their feet as hard as they could to make the ghost go away.

While they were scaring each other one very dark night, Jan called out,

"I can hear galloping. Oh it's getting louder and louder. Be quiet everyone!"

The children fell silent and listened and sure enough they all heard the galloping. It was coming towards the house. They all crouched down and peered out the window, into the darkness. The shadowy figures of two horsemen appeared. One was slumped over his horse and they both had guns.

Nonnie went outside and they heard her speaking to them in their own language. So the children knew they were Commandos and were no longer afraid. The men had come from the battle where they had been fighting with Nonnie's husband, who was an important General in the Commandos. One soldier was wounded in the shoulder from a bullet.

The first thing Nonnie did was take care of the wounded soldier who was bleeding. She bandaged his arm and made a sling.

The Commandos then told Nonnie some sad news.

Her farmhouse, which she'd left behind, had been burned down by Khakis some weeks ago. Everyone felt so very sad about this news and Nonnie cried for a little while. Nonnie was always so brave and cheerful and now the children were upset to see her tears.

But some time later, Nonnie dried her eyes and said she was still grateful that they hadn't been captured and put in a prison camp.

"We are lucky to be here, and to still have food to eat. Before these good soldiers leave us to fight again, we must give them a good healthy meal. Chicken casserole is just what they need to make them strong."

Oh no, thought Koos. I don't want chicken for dinner. He needed to think fast.

When no one was looking he found Cluck in the coop, popped her into the sack and hid her where she wouldn't be found.

CHAPTER 13

The Very Strange Ghost

The third night after the soldiers arrived, the children were again playing spooky games in the dark. Jan said the ghost of the spotted leopard had returned and they could see its shadow on the wall, its eyes glinting yellow in the dark. The children were yelling and stomping their feet to frighten it away and the soldiers joined in.

From down the dark, empty hallway they heard

thumping. They stopped shouting and listened. Annie felt her heart thumping. Susanna peered around the corner down the hallway and she could see something jolting about. Trembling, she grabbed Jan's hand and pulled him to the doorway. Then all was quiet as they peered into the dark. Oh yes, there it was again, jolting from side to side, thumping and banging. This wasn't a shadow from the firelight, this was something moving and thumping. Perhaps it was the ghost of Grandfather Makim looking for his rocking chair.

Even the soldiers did not look courageous. The tall soldier went to find his gun, but Koos called out, "You can't shoot a ghost because it is already dead!"

But the soldier came back with his gun and aimed it down the hall straight towards where the ghost was jolting about. Quickly, Koos grabbed the gun and yelled, "No, don't shoot, let me catch the ghost."

Nobody could believe their eyes as Koos ran down the hallway and grabbed the ghost. It was moving in his arms as he returned to the kitchen.

"Now Cluck don't be afraid," he said, as he reached into the sack and lifted out his pet chicken and put her protectively under his arm.

Nonnie understood at once. It all made sense

now. That was why there was an extra chicken in the coop, that was why Koos was always getting bugs and beetles, and that was why he always wanted to help with the chickens. He had smuggled his pet on to the wagon and was taking care of it. Her face was as black as thunder.

She said, "Koos you are a disobedient child and I think we should eat Cluck for dinner tomorrow. She will be very tasty and everyone will enjoy eating her."

"Oh no," said Koos "she won't be tasty, not with all those tockie tock beetles, grubs and grasshoppers inside her, she'll taste disgusting and everyone will get tummy ache."

"Please, Nonnie," begged Annie "Koos is the youngest here and he needs his pet chicken. He will be broken-hearted without her."

Both the soldiers agreed that Koos should keep his chicken and neither of them wanted to eat the boy's pet. Nonnie still looked angry but agreed not to kill Cluck. They ate another chicken and everyone was happy. The next morning the soldiers left to return to the battlefield.

CHAPTER 14

Crossing the Harts River

Two days later the soldiers galloped back to the house and said, "Nonnie, you cannot stay here. The enemy troops are coming this way and you must leave tomorrow." Then the soldiers rode away. This was a warning for them to move quickly.

Again the wagons were packed and, at first light, they were on their way. It was very cold and a storm was coming, but there was no time to worry about such

things. Along the trek there were many other families on their wagons all going towards the Harts River.

The sky was black. Suddenly, lightning flashed, there was a crash of thunder, silence followed, then huge drops of rain fell. They beat against the canvas on the wagon where the children were sheltering. The rain was so loud that the children couldn't hear each other even when they were shouting as loudly as they could.

Nonnie's wagons were the first to reach the river. The wagons creaked as the oxen dragged them down the steep slope of the riverbank. The children had to get out of the wagon while the oxen pulled as hard as they could. It was such a heavy load.

The children were cold and the rain was beating in their faces. Inkoshi said to hold tight to the side of the wagon and step carefully into the river. The river was not very deep, but it was running swiftly. Annie could feel her long skirt being pulled by the water.

"I can't hold on any longer," she yelled.

Quickly Koos grabbed a rope hanging from the wagon. Jan grabbed his outstretched arm. With his other hand he grabbed Annie's skirt. They formed a human chain. Gradually, Jan was able to pull Annie closer towards him. There they stood in the middle of the river unable to move. Annie's clothes were long, sodden with water and very heavy. She was shivering and frightened. She held Jan's hand but he couldn't move.

Above the sound of the raging storm he yelled, "Inkoshi, Msizi, help us, help us."

The men climbed around the wagon until they reached Koos, then climbed down into the water. They held Koos, then Jan and finally were able to grab Annie passing her back from one to the other until they reached the wagon. Msizi climbed onto the back of the wagon and then Inkoshi pushed Annie up into his arms. She was now very cold but safe on the wagon.

The oxen pulled hard through the water and the first wagon moved up the slope of the riverbank on the other side. The oxen pulled but were very tired and Inkoshi cracked his whip to drive them on.

The mud was sucking at their legs. The lead ox fell and was pulled to his feet by Jan, Inkoshi and Msizi. The wagon moved out of the river but its wheels became stuck in the mud.

All the while, Annie was lying in the back of the covered wagon trying to get warm under her quilt. She could hear the groaning of the wagon as it was dragged through river. She felt it lurch as the pots and pans clattered about.

She felt the wagon stop and could hear the men shouting and the whips cracking. Annie wondered what was happening. Just as she looked out the back, Koos climbed up to her and said, "We are stuck in the mud! Nonnie says we need help quickly to dig the wheels out, but we can only wait until the men from the other wagons can help us. I am so hungry and I'm not good at waiting."

It was growing dark when they heard the voices of strangers. Four big men were approaching with spades. Annie and Koss climbed down the back of the wagon to watch. The men used their spades and some wood to lift the wheels out of the mud, then Inkoshi cracked his whip and the oxen pulled the wagon onto the dry land. The second wagon followed, and at last they continued on their way.

CHAPTER 15

The Night Sky

Nonnie's wagons were the first to cross the river, followed by the wagons of many other families, trying to escape the Khakis. There were about twelve wagons following each other along the track to Badenhorst in the dark and all the people were cold and wet. It was difficult to continue but they couldn't stop until they found some dry, open ground where they could camp. Finally they found a large area where there was soft grass and surrounding trees. The first rays of sunshine rose above the trees and cast long shadows. The wanderers were very weary as they made camp. The wagons formed a circle, as men, women and children gathered together. Annie and Koos joined other children to look for firewood before they could rest.

Before long, a fire was lit and the women put their big casserole pots over the embers to cook breakfast and make coffee. Everyone gathered around to dry their soggy clothes and boots. Many of the eggs that Nonnie had saved had broken during the river crossing but the Van Bellen family had spare eggs which they were pleased to give to Nonnie. Nonnie made two huge omelettes which she shared amongst the families.

After breakfast the children lay under the shade of the wagons to rest on the soft grass. Koos let the chickens out to peck around the place. It was very peaceful and most of the wanderers fell asleep until late in the afternoon. Their clothes had dried and before long it was time to prepare dinner.

Looking up into the sky that night, the wanderers saw the stars in all their brilliance. Annie knew this was what she loved most. She wondered how all those stars got in the sky and why some sparkled but others shone. One day she would find out, but for

now she just wanted to stare and imagine she was flying through the dark up, up, to the brightest star.

When Jan played his harmonica and all the wanderers sang, she thought how much she loved being under the night sky. As she looked up, a huge yellow ball with a long tail, blazed across the darkness and Annie could not believe her eyes

"It's a comet," Nonnie called. "Let's hope that it brings us good luck."

Koos said, "I don't think its going to crash into the veldt. It's going the wrong way. Maybe it's going to America. Maybe people over there will see it too."

Never before had the wanderers seen anything like this. They had seen many shooting stars but this was different. The comet continued to move across the sky in an arc, but did not fall downwards like a shooting star.

During the next three nights the comet appeared on the dark horizon. But it did not bring them luck as Nonnie hoped.

CHAPTER 16

Leaving the Harts River

During the third night of the passing comet, Annie and Koos were on their camp bed talking about the comet and wondering if Mother and their brothers and baby sister saw the comet in the south. Perhaps they also looked up into the night sky and saw the comet and thought about Annie and Koos. They snuggled under their quilt and talked about the things they would tell Mumma and Father when they saw them.

Just before morning, Koos heard a terrible noise coming from the chicken coop. Without doubt there were hyenas yowling and calling and this could mean only one thing. They were trying to get the chickens! Leaping from the bed and grabbing his slingshot, Koos peered through the opening of the tent and saw the shape of three spotted hyenas stalking back and forward near the coop. Perched on top of the coop was a chicken, which was most upset and clucking with fright. It was not Cluck, but Koos knew he had to rescue her from these ugly creatures.

From where he was standing, the hyenas could not see him. He took a smooth stone from his pocket, placed it in the pouch of the slingshot and whirled it above his head aiming in the direction of the hyenas. Just at the right moment he released the stone, which shot through the air hitting a hyena on its hind leg. With a mighty yowl of pain the hyena limped away into the bushes followed by the other two creatures.

"Oh great shot Koos, I didn't think you could do it" called Jan, and Annie ran to kiss her brother. She felt so proud of him and Koos felt pretty proud of himself.

When breakfast time came, the children were not so happy. There was not much to eat and they were hungry. And still Nonnie said they must be on their way before the Khakis found them. The oxen were yoked, the wagons loaded and they were on their way again along the sandy track.

They could hear the sound of cannons not far away and before long a Commando horseman approached the wagon. He had news of the battle and said, "We've captured General Smith an important leader of the Khakis. He is wounded and lying in a tent not far from where we now are."

Nonnie said she would see this man, for she had been told that he had given the orders for her farmhouse to be burned and she wanted to talk to him. The Commando took Nonnie to General Smith and Annie went along with them, bringing some medicine and bandages.

Nonnie felt very angry with this man, because he had given the orders for her farmhouse to be burned. When she entered the tent he was lying on his camp bed with his wounded leg still bleeding and he looked very weak. It was not the right time for angry words. Annie brought out the bandages and antiseptic and Nonnie used them to treat the wounded man. She left without saying any of the things she wanted to say to him.

CHAPTER 17

Nonnie, Annie and The General

The next day Nonnie and Annie returned to the tent where General Smith was being held prisoner. He was still very weak but he was pleased to see Nonnie and Annie and thanked them for their help. It was now time for Nonnie to ask the questions that were on her mind. Annie sat and listened.

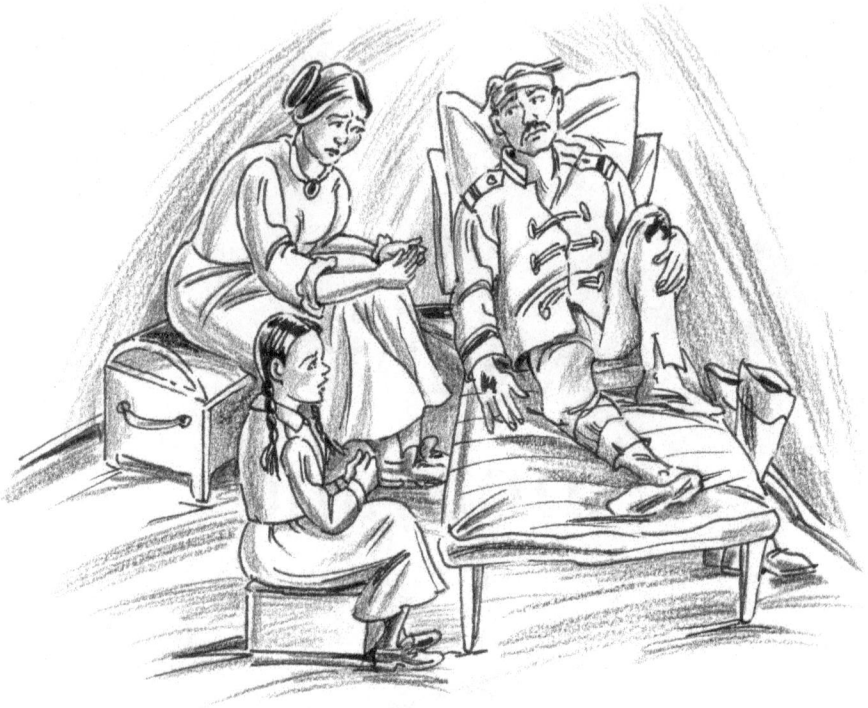

"You burned my farmhouse and Annie's farm house, General Smith, and I want to understand why you did this," she asked.

"You are right, Madam, I did give orders for the farmhouses to be burned, and for this I feel truly sorry. We were worried that your husband and the other Commando soldiers would return for food and supplies. For us to win the war, we needed to stop the supplies." He looked at Nonnie and Annie and then continued, "War is a terrible thing and it makes men do things they don't want to do."

"Yes" said Nonnie, "you seem like a kind, gentle man and it is a shame that you did these things to win a war. You must have known it would cause suffering but still you did it. Now you are our prisoner and I'm not sure that the Commandos will set you free."

Nonnie then said, "My husband is riding here from the battlefield tomorrow. He is a very important Commando and I will ask him to set you free to return to England. You have apologised to me and I accept that you did these things because of the war, and because of what you felt you had to do."

All the while Annie listened and thought much about kind people doing terrible things just because there was a war. Nonnie and Annie then left the General, shaking hands with him and wishing him good luck.

How strange it seemed to be shaking hands with the enemy when they were still at war with that same enemy.

The next day Nonnie's husband arrived from the battle field. He had with him the two Commandos whom the wanderers had met at the Makim farmhouse. Another large group of Commandos arrived a short time later. Nonnie explained to her husband that General Smith had apologised for burning down their house and she argued that he should be set free. Her husband thought about this and agreed, but the other Commandos disagreed. Finally, two days later and after much argument they all decided to let General Smith return to England.

Annie and Nonnie returned to their wagons and the wanderers continued further along the track, but it was becoming more and more difficult. There was not enough food. It was also difficult to find enough firewood to keep themselves warm and to keep the lions from their camp at night.

It was on one of these very cold nights, when the wind was lashing the canvas covered wagons that a horseman arrived with news. They gathered about to hear what he had to say.

"The war is over, we must surrender to the Khakis. They have won and we have lost," he said.

CHAPTER 18

A Bitter Peace, but Peace at Last

Although the children didn't really understand why it was so terrible, they knew that their side, the side of the Commandos, had lost the war. Nonnie's children as well as Annie and Koos cried to think that their fathers had fought bravely but lost. They also cried because their homes had been burned and that now there was nowhere to go but back to their empty land and ruined houses.

They asked Nonnie what had this war meant, now that they were the losers. Nonnie explained that now the King of the British people was their ruler. The British now had control of their land and could decide many things that they might not agree with. But they were now free to go back to their farms.

And this is what happened. The wagon turned around and they headed back to Lichtenberg to Nonnie's farm. They found there was one building still standing amongst the ruins. There was at least some shelter until they could rebuild.

Annie and Koos stayed on with Nonnie waiting for their mother to return from the south and for their father to return to their farm. One morning, they saw a small cart approach Nonnie's place, and there was Father sitting in the driver's seat. Oh, how wonderful it was to see him!

As he climbed down from the cart they could see something was wrong with his leg. He limped towards them with his big brown arms open wide and tears in his eyes. Annie and Koos hugged him tightly and didn't want to let go.

Father turned to Nonnie and said, "You have been so kind to take care of Annie and Koos and I will look forward to hearing about all their adventures with you, but now I must take them back to our place where their mother is waiting."

Nonnie hugged them and their cousins called goodbye as they climbed on the cart. Annie shook hands with Inkoshi and Msizi and thanked them for taking care of her. Koos tucked Cluck under his arm and they set off along the same track they had come with Mother in the carriage so long before.

They reached the gate of their farm and saw that their house was ruined. The roof had been burned and the walls had crumbled. A large tent had been set up and outside the tent two boys were playing. Koos and Annie shouted their brothers' names and they came running to them, jumping and shouting back.

Mumma was waiting inside the tent with a little girl who was running and squealing with excitement. This must be the baby sister they left behind. Mumma stood with her arms open wide and a huge smile on her face.

"Oh" said Annie, "this is just a tent but it feels like home because we're all together again." She reached into her apron pocket and brought out her doll, Polly, and gave it to her little sister. She felt too grown up to have a doll now.

Later that night while they sat around the fire,

Annie brought out her sketchbook and showed Mother and Father her drawings of the honey bird, the elephants and the comet. Mumma said that they were so interesting and so well done, that one day Annie could have art lessons.

Father said that Annie had talent and he would make picture frames for her drawings. But first of all they needed to build a new house because he said, "You can't possibly hang pictures in a tent." And Koos knew he would help Father build a new house.

And so it was, O Best Beloved, that a new farmhouse

was built for the Greeff Family with many rooms and a long veranda where they would all sit at night looking at the stars and talking about the time the comet streaked across the darkness.